THE LAST PREDICTA

Crab Orchard Series in Poetry

Editor's Selection

THE LAST PREDICTA

CHAD DAVIDSON

Crab Orchard Review

&

Southern Illinois University Press

CARBONDALE

11   10   09   08   4   3   2   1

The Crab Orchard Series in Poetry is a joint publishing venture of
Southern Illinois University Press and *Crab Orchard Review*. This
series has been made possible by the generous support of the Office
of the President of Southern Illinois University and the Office of the
Vice Chancellor for Academic Affairs and Provost at Southern Illinois
University Carbondale.

Crab Orchard Series in Poetry Editor: Jon Tribble

Library of Congress Cataloging-in-Publication Data

Davidson, Chad, 1970–

The last predicta / Chad Davidson.

p. cm. — (Crab Orchard series in poetry)

ISBN-13: 978-0-8093-2875-8 (pbk. : alk. paper)

ISBN-10: 0-8093-2875-5 (pbk. : alk. paper)

I. Title.

PS3604.A946L37   2008

811'.6—dc22   2008005835

Printed on recycled paper. ♻

The paper used in this publication meets the minimum requirements
of American National Standard for Information Sciences—Permanence
of Paper for Printed Library Materials, ANSI Z39.48-1992. ∞

FOR GWEN

Farewell my friends, I go to glory!

—ISADORA DUNCAN

Contents

FOUR

Acknowledgments

Grateful acknowledgment is made to the editors of the following publications, in which poems from this book first appeared, though sometimes in different form:

AGNI—"Rosy-Fingered Whatever" and "Tokyo: A Parable"
Artful Dodge—"Worms"
Barrow Street—"The Death of Byron"
Beloit Poetry Journal—"Flies"
Birmingham Poetry Review—"Scavengers"
Chattahoochee Review—"American Cheerleader" and "Nostos"
Crab Orchard Review—"Advent"
Cream City Review—"Astricide" and "Small Deaths"
Elixir—"Starburst"
Epoch—"The Wanderer State"
Green Mountains Review—"Golden-Clad Something Nice"
Hiram Poetry Review—"Pseudoscorpion"
Hotel Amerika—"Diva"
Isotope—"Opossum"
Kennesaw Review—"Dead Swans" and "Idol"
Lake Effect—"The Divine"
Mid-American Review—"This Entire Minute"
Mississippi Review—"Bird's Eye"
The National Poetry Review—"Fever"
Passages North—"The Big Spill," "Gold's Gym," and "Target"
Prairie Schooner—"The Calling of St. Matthew: X-Ray Photograph"
Shenandoah—"The Tiniest Green Hummingbird in the World"
Smartish Pace—"Beheading Bacchus"
32 Poems Magazine—"Carnival," "Stardom," and "The Beginning"
Virginia Quarterly Review—"The Last Predicta TV"

"Diva," "Flies," and "Target" are reprinted on *From the Fishouse: An Audio Archive of Emerging Poets* (www.fishousepoems.org).

Thanks to the Sewanee Writer's Conference, especially Wyatt Prunty and Cheri Peters, for a generous Walter E. Dakin Fellowship. Thanks to my teachers—Bruce Bond, B. H. Fairchild, Robert Hass, and Austin Hummell. Thanks to my friends, especially Jane and Bob Hill, Leslie McGrath, Erika Meitner, and Eric Smith, for being careful readers time and again. Thanks to Allison Joseph, Jon Tribble, and all the people at Southern Illinois University Press. Thanks to my family, always. Finally, special thanks to Greg Fraser and John Poch, whose friendship, patience, and knowledge resulted in your reading this right now.

ONE

Target

Dear Arrowhead water, dear feather boa, dear father
and mother with the toddler and cart full of candles:

I wanted to tell you the sky swished open its doors
this morning, the whole shebang slid by on felt,

and I entered the mythic fires of stoicism,
bore my nakedness in the manner of Shackleton,

defiantly ignorant. For I know that Target, centerless
like new pedagogies, loves the good good,

loves punishment somehow instructing
a niche audience. That's me. I love to finger

the Milano-style whatnot, bend the necks
of five-headed floor lamps. Yes, I love you dearly,

dear church of the cherished storage bin,
dear Cheerios and the bowl to drown you in,

dear warehouse sky, dear reindeer aiming the beads
of your eyes at my impulse buys. Once, I shot a gun

in the desert, laid it down in the sand, and said
a small prayer to prayers of small sizes.

Years later, we navigated the marked-downs,
the Doritos safe in Mylar pillows,

thought we'd stripped ourselves clean
of desire's burrs and foxtails, even as popcorn

promised low-sodium transubstantiation.
But we were *registering*, the word itself green, bearded,

so aimed our fantastic machines at the crock
pot and bath rug, at the iPod snug in its skin.

We dressed ourselves in the warmth of that small space
heater, fed the nuisance of class consciousness

little biscuits. How cloudless, how terrible and lucid
the distances we traveled for our dear wedding guests—

dear, which my Italian friend uses in that foreign way,
as in, *That pair of pants is too dear.* And how dear, how sheer

the night, we thought, dearly beloved, outside the Target,
the headlights of all those cars trained on us.

Gold's Gym

Mounting the stationary bike, you bear witness
to Sheila in her leotard amid an hour's worth
of miniature death, her heart rapping on its chamber door.
You've traveled beyond the distant water
fountain, beyond the sauna crying its salt on the floor,

have been conveyed nowhere in twenty minutes,
the eighteenth green dangling before you in simulcast.
Warmed up, you scoff at the fat guy in the small car
of a hack-squat machine, load-bearing and ridiculous,
while Christina Aguilera taunts from the far shore

of her pop song, indigenous, bland as a high school
witch club. Would it have been better to split
some logs, build a pyre, sacrifice some self
to the arrival of the great black gym suits ghosting
through midnight on local TV, guaranteeing weight

loss without loss? Just think of the iconography,
of the Gatorade with its Technicolor flavors,
its promise of the eternal spring and jump shot.
Before the Nile, when bodies were not temples
so much as atriums, the small finch of the heart

banged its cage to bear witness. Bruises were small ponds
our histories swam in. Given time, the white robes
of Renaissance women's flesh unfurled down the walls
of museums in which we ran, room to room, breathless
for their leisure. Was there never the remotest chance

of becoming purer, browned and trained by the sun
with its legion of torturers? Must we live in our bodies
and punish them, too? Towel off, Sheila, and grab your keys.
Because late, when the tattoos have hunkered in their sleeves,
and the herds of duffel bags by the coat rack have cleared,

and each straggler recollects the pain the body knows
as good and true—as good as water, as true as water torture—
in the black moons of plates skewered on their pegs
a calmness wells, imperceptible, loving, finally radiant,
as the monitors flat-line and the loudspeaker calls out:

Dear patrons: You are all, like us, dying. The moon that ruptures
each night in the drowsy winters of our windows is not faking.
We will see you tomorrow, or the next day, or the next.
Be mindful that we see you, even through the coastal fog
your body manufactures. And we will help you to the shore.

American Cheerleader

Trojans never dreamed the Helenesque
pomp she pom-poms for, teasing the eagle
mascot in his turtleneck fraught with thirst.
(Through his beak, he eyes the jugs of Gatorade.)

Neither did they think beyond the lust
of lone Achilles, to the thousands spectating
from ramparts, wailing, waving to their lovers
on the killing field, infant in the crook of an arm.

So this is life, Cassandra says. Cheerleading is nothing
if not naked prophecy, platonic on those beds
of turf unreal enough we imagine grayer grass
on Elysium. The quarterback breaks the huddle,

purples the pigskin with fear and fingerprints,
while she calls behind the stone symmetry
of linebackers declaring it good—her hepped-up chant
channeling them to yellow we all see through

the augur of instant replay. This, the greatest challenge
to Western metaphysics, appears weekly in coliseums
and the eyes of TVs walling a sports bar, at the end
of cul-de-sacs elegiacally named: Fern Hollow, Quail Run.

There, there. How could Greeks have known grief, too,
flows from the embers of a simulcast, into living rooms
cavernous, leatherclad, into the cheerleader commuting
in pressed rayon? For every open space, the battle

and sheen of the cheer, window dressing we all peer at
(and through) to catch sight of ourselves—the great
unnumbered—awaiting one last pass of the Blue
Angels, not some baggy blimp pimping the end.

Diva

The very veery this heart thumps for,
she seems a mere heartbeat away,
a buoy bobbing in a bay

on whose shores I sit tongue-tied
to the sound of a fishing boat
tonguing the soft-sand shore-lap.

It's March. And if I reel it in,
it is real. So to step in,
swivel dingy oarlocks and plod

out nearer the buoy seems
the very act of throating a bird
as one might stroke a chicken neck

to pacify. Isadora Duncan
knows (or knew) all too well
this feather-fingering of Fate,

both divas. Stay with me.
I am moving quite fast, sculling
by the buoy before I know it

as the very emblem of the veery
I would like each chatty bird
in this narrative to be.

Stay with me, croons the buoy
Bette-Midlerian as I scull by
thwartwise. Thickets rise

out of the shore muck starboard,
my skull now heavy with chirping.
Stay with me, and I'd like to

slip out and slide to the spout
end of that buoy throatwise
and risen to song. *This is weird*,

I tell myself, by which I mean
the Anglo-Saxon kind, which kills
the very veery my heart adores.

Heart, if you have the heart,
help me swing the dinghy round.
We have but one tongue between us.

Stardom

Hello, says your chauffeur, accent on the *o*, as in,
O how the ice bin sweats. Now look you've gone
and let him break your resolve to peek at the mini
bar's free what-have-yous or solve the moon-

roof sheer and blue as a nightgown's underside.
The tequila-sunrise sun, cherryless but cheery,
fizzles in its sky-blue highball, and you'd just as soon
be a sequin in the pool of your lap, wading

beneath the palms, waving to fans at the fern bar.
(They are drinking a drink named after your name.)
So this, you think, is what the butterfly feels
atop the Hollywood Bowl: *Hello, hell.* Soon,

you'll be whisked away to Barbados, dissolved
into the glossy of a gaggle of flashbulbs, lovers
all, saying open your eyes wide and say *whiskey*.
Your body's grown a gown around that word.

Rosy-Fingered Whatever

Few things convince like the Greek landscape
in Dörpfeld's 1900 translation of *The Odyssey*,
dawn sprawling on its doily of cumuli as a lover
might a bed not hers. Or now, amazed as windows,

our eyes the wine-blue of water with nothing below,
we keep blotting the boo-boo of you—revenant,
radiant in gauze. Each day, Persephone-etched,
you return to a number, dumber each time

the date falls like a date: too soft, honeyed to solvency.
Edible erasure, you could peek from the corners of a sunset,
or star as a new star scarring the night's black bay
above Los Angeles. We can see it all now,

all of you. If only the clouds would tear asunder.
At least unclasp. Just say you'll hang around, wave
to the waves the first surfer craves as he lounges
in the broken hourglass of his ritual, rubbing wax.

Carnival

Fresh rock lobster and rock climbing and classic rock
live every Saturday in the captain's ballroom,
and for no one in particular the eventual opening
of the suckling pig. Back up into the Cadillac

ice sculpture and the stewards will open the doors
to your latest apocalypse. Best case scenario? All is lost,
the conjunction *and* recovers its biblical connotations,
while everyone helps themselves to more

of those Easter strawberries thank you very much.
Near boardwalks under which no one by law may sit,
shoeless fishermen sally forth with the faces of shoes.
The spriteless jetty unspirals into computer-enhanced

post-ocean. A dance number bleeds from lungs
atop the Hilton, something about a *corazón* going out
to Sally and her husband who come here for the vanilla.
Back when the beaches of islands frowned like bananas,

some Simon inspected the cracks of an idol's smile,
pulled a chalk bag out and spanked his hands
as a magician might, or a mighty short stop, thinking,
O my shoes, o for a face for a face for a face.

Starburst

On the corner of every disaster
lies a small store selling gasoline,
coffee, cigarette lighters, Starburst.
The distasteful car-wax display may
double as your cardboard funerary.
NASCAR scars the magazine racks.

Like the American finch, building
its nest so tight its nestlings drown
in storms, the small store heaves against
the coffee-heavy air of 7 A.M.
with the persistence of the ambulance
blasting Skynyrd in the lot.

On the sidewalk of every disaster
a star burns her prints into cement
and signs there, sings to the child
in us all who wishes for life
less punctuated by stars burning
into the earth, burning out.

Like the Empire State Building
of over ninety movies, including
Godzilla and *King Kong,* we are
the hinge stardom swivels on.
Like the Empire State Building . . .
Wait. That *is* the Empire State Building.

On the disaster of every coroner
discovering how the lot of us die, we say,
Where went the bloodless microscopy
of television and Carl Sagan? The answer
comes from the ambulance with ambivalence:
Every hour is the autopsy of a second.

TWO

Golden-Clad Something Nice

Pardon the gazpacho Ferrari-colored on Formica and the brie sinking into itself like quicksand by the sink. I didn't think you'd mind competing flavors. For you, I've put the flies to sleep. The birds may watch TV. The willow weeps for you outside. I've bought an inexpensive tapioca for dessert. In the desert, children of Ethiopia spin naked in their shadows like tops on a Testarossa. No worries. The seven-layer dip is just like your mother used to make. When I was young, I made a bird of my hands and let it flap on the ground and die. No, that was this morning. Ten pounds of tomatoes I cooked for you. Funny how erasure tastes good. This is where sonnets normally end. Instead, we are having a nice time. I saw a special once: a city in Spain where inhabitants fight with tomatoes. I'm not sure if any birds were injured during filming. Imagine throttling your pathetic car through that city on that day, the film crew looking on, the tomato in the hand of every single person in that city just for you. For now, I shall bring you a crouton, which, if you don't know, is the diminutive of *crust*.

This Entire Minute

A thousand die in a good day. Obediently,
the great ice-cube maker spits out its countable
nothing, each minute easing into the next

so seamless we set our clocks to even
the most meager of hearts, boxy like a Volvo
or Japanese watermelon. Sixty make an hour

with its air of possession, or the TV news
keeping time by its aging anchor. Propped
in the green room taking five, he practices the hand

sweep that brings us giddy to the next
commercial. To witness the birth of an entire minute:
the first tentative seconds give way to slower,

surer ones through which the minute may achieve
self-actualization, dissolution into the future,
where it resembles us most—this yearning to be

out of time with all the time in the world.
In early times, before light bulbs and dyspepsia,
days sped by like honest comets, burning

our image into backlit cactuses, each long stalk
an hour hand. Now days move with the chill
of glaciers, carving their names into our sponge-

like cognizance. What do we care, now that each
second weighs enough to merit kick-backs
just to keep on keeping on? Give us the good days

and the Brady Bunch who aged sixty minutes each week.
Legions, agile, quick to arm, line up inside
the nearest clock to prove themselves temporal again.

And the thought of them advancing to this
particular moment—this entire minute we know
we're living in this day—becomes our only consolation.

Because somewhere, we're convinced, someone
already lived this entire minute in which a woman
in Japan revels in the perfection of a watermelon—

the watermelon she slices, this watermelon, here,
and the black seeds pregnant with possibility,
aching for their hour, which passed some time ago.

The Last Predicta TV

Martians, for instance, in their metal Frisbee
appeared from no less immaculate
chrome borders themselves
spit-shined like Art Deco

mirrors. A Pyramus and Thisbe
for the increasingly illiterate,
packed in shotgun houses like shelves,
1959 and '60 carried their cargo

of oracles and relevant trivia:
the Philco model 4371
sported a sixteen-inch screen
swiveling on a smug, Chevy-like

chassis, while the sports trivium
of baseball-football-baseball won
over even wives and pimply teens
hungry as they were for barlight,

green men, no-hitters: in short,
anything that shines,
anything that makes things
easy, seamless, slow to burn.

Picture my father, the sort
that buys a car and keeps it, whines
over nothing save his lawn and engine pings,
only eighteen when the last wheel turned

on the Predicta assembly.
He's looking into the future
of TV, a future continually there
an hour before he arrives

with popcorn, soft drink, and me,
or some version of me, in the aperture.
We're a seam that wants to tear,
he and I, that Predicta, and the lives

blooming there in Technicolor.
For each new generation a new genus
and the genius who named it,
who foretold the dangers

the widely cultivated horror
of solid state circuitry would be to us
who lived by the conduit,
cast in the die of predictable strangers.

The Wanderer State

Back when the sky was the color of your father
in his blue Chevy exiled in the forgettable desert
east of L.A., back when sculptors figured
every body's worth by the time it took
to freeze one into memory's marbled forests,
we petrified each other so lovingly
you thought I was sky-blue, effortless
as a bad tattoo. So if you find me chatting
to the face of a clock as some Susannah
fingers her wrist and whispers *rutabaga*—
or is it *rhododendron*?—know I mean no meanness.
Recall that Rodin—French sculptor scared of France—
could almost be a giant bird over Japan
where surly teens wear t-shirts tattooed
with the slogans of the dispossessed—
Yippee Cola Boy, Good Girl Sky.
Good girl. Goodnight. Good clock to wash away
the night. Do you see? If you repeat my name
in a closet I'll begin a study of the saddest fugue,
and you'll listen for what seems like hours
until some Susannah, emergent émigré from Indiana—
the wanderer state—flashes a breast
below which a caption reads, simply, *Love me.*

Worms

Just as the butler-passed puff pastries, salmon-laden
on a polished platter, slip from the living room's saddened

mahogany to mingling richies, we will evade you.
Poolside with a stupid boyfriend named Stu

after mindless sex, you tip earthward your faux
fedora to our tiny interrogative bodies you know

will die on the pavement you dare not walk with bare feet.
Not wholly part of this world, vermiculate,

tongues ourselves, we taper, nonetheless, to a stub, like a ticket
or last night's dinner conversation. If you can make it,

meet us on the terrace when the over-watered ficus
spills. Or, while repairing polo divots, mimic us—

fleshy, spirited as any horse haunch, chicken neck, gecko's
tail. And though we screw like Archimedes, lick the spit off stilettos,

in the snake of a body on the shower floor,
you may find yourself staring too long. Finger,

annelid, we wear your indiscretion
like wedding-ring mold. The decision

is yours. Stu awaits somewhere, holding a tray
heavy with faux fruit and cheese spread. Already,

you can feel the lump in his pocket where you know
squirms the ring he'd love to thread on you.

Astricide

If you drift starboard, find the wheel and throw
both hands portward far enough to break the bowstride.
If there's slack in your jib, merely cheer as Romans did,
who lacked the god and subsequent fear of dying stars.

Because when you fall—and you will—you traipse
barren fields in a shroud of Nordic fog. Enshrined there,
the Teutonic build of your assassin reminds you of a sea
filled with dead fish and story, the scarier for the darker

spots. His name is hoary: *Thor* or *Sven*. Just then,
a killer whale breaches. Starboard, a single star—
before he turns the axe downward, or sword across
your throat—burns too brightly, toggles off.

And you die like that: clean, puffed up from battle
or the semblance of. Should you wake to the horizon
stiff as the first iron mast, search out
some tattered thread of coast. The languor

of your craft will will your fears to you
in legion. Keep limber. Make the shrill gull
your keeper. Regions you never thought existed
come like hip, unlisted ports to a cruise ship.

In the meantime, enjoy the sloth, the dry Martini
in a pool, the dress cut low, far too tiny
to cover all the swells of her body: huge hips,
breasts that rose and fell, it seemed, with that huge ship,

far too huge to notice you: guppy in a kiddie pool,
cod in Rome, a novice, a drifter a tad off pole.

Tokyo: A Parable

There is a bar in Tokyo where sushi arrives on the plate of a naked woman. There is a Tokyo in sushi, microbes in microbe high-rises, where the plate of a naked woman arrives on a bar in a bar named for some ridiculous fish or movie star. When Tokyo arrives, I hail her with my shorn chopsticks now resting on the plate of a naked woman named for some ridiculous fish or movie star. On a bar in a bar named for the city that birthed it, naked women rest on their white fainting couches waiting for Tokyo to arrive. I hail with my movie stars and fish, puffing my ridiculous chest. High-rises rise around the bar in a bar, like naked women. Wait. They *are* naked women. Wait, Tokyo. Don't go. A weight rests on my naked chest like a plate of sushi or a bad tattoo. It is the profile of you, naked, that arrives on the horizon of my chest as a freckle constellation, or the bubbles a fish puffs on the fainting couch of a sand bar's slow strangle, whose arrival a woman on the shore hails with her naked knife. And if she is ridiculously hungry, her name is Tokyo.

THREE

The Calling of St. Matthew: X-Ray Photograph

Call it a gift, Christ's opening the mouth
of the room with a hand. As if it could speak.
Overhead, an ellipse, left imperfect, hovers.

Beardless men flare their peacock sleeves,
offer the face of the money table their silk.
Under a lamp of paint, they have come

to count on their friend's sudden departure,
as we have, minutes before closing, arrived
with an unexpected flock of school children,

the live silica of their voices sifting through
the air around us in this darkened chapel
a short walk from the Pantheon, where you noticed

what looked like mortar blasts in the inscription
to Agrippa. I slide another coin into the spotlight's slot,
and Matthew has never seen so far into the faces

of coins. Still, he catches Christ's hand horizonward,
bending the currency of his stare, as students close
around the canvas, the clicks and flashes of cameras

bruising the gift of our last day in Rome. Earlier,
under the ocular lens of the Pantheon, we counted
the centuries before the invention of photography,

imagined Agrippa grasping the spade that laid its face down
first in the dirt where his monument now faces
the faces of millions, in millions of photos per year.

Earlier still, we searched every tourist shop
a mile from here for an early photo of the Pantheon
and found it—women in full dress, horse and carriage

tethered to the pillars' enormity. Men wore hats.
You thought early 1900s. Why do we return?
Back at San Luigi, with the Pantheon rolled

in its cardboard scepter, I point towards St. Peter—
fingerprint, luscious smudge—whom x-rays prove
is a present, an afterthought in this painting's party

whose end is also its future, where food never rests
on the table, never will. You shush the students
and they stare with the astonishment of martyrs.

People once died for art. For less. For the last time
today, the spotlight's eye closes. The students disband,
one waving from the door mouth, stalled, throwing

his hand across the face of the floor, like Christ's hand
behind the late addition of St. Peter. This all occurs,
by the way, thousands of years after the first image

of Christ was burned into the catacombs of San Sebastiano.
And if it's true that among his apprentices Caravaggio
kept a lover, one he painted over and over, we imagine

the boy in his own eternal celebrity, oiled by the inevitable
camera flash burning him deeper into the church
our coming here has made of this day. Late autumn now.

The sun chokes on the fishbones of TV antennae
and, though dimmed, sifts through thoroughfares,
charging the cobblestones under us.

Scavengers

A Victorian gentleman and the skeleton
of a stork in this daguerreotype bathed
in bone and silver. Argentine, jaundiced,
his arm near the ludicrous beak, as if it too could

swallow geometry. *We can only be so naked,*
the image declares to a wall or a wallet without
photos. In a photo, dated 1920, my grandfather,
younger than I am now, on a beach where everyone

wears black and an easy despair nurtured
by science. Everyone loves necessarily the sight
of the sea, and to be empurpled by such enormity
of water makes them all scavengers.

A few gulls spread over the foam.
Sandpipers relay. A sham, the winter
this photograph tells me of, as my grandfather
rumples the brim of a hat that cannot be his.

In seconds he will toss it into the onlookers
like a spider web their faces discover as they walk
through the early twentieth century to me. History
is a word developed for fear of our own enormity.

No. Too heavy-handed. Because I, like
the Victorian gentleman at his flying museum,
stare at my grandfather and his people
pushed to the edge and gathered there.

They are part of an idea of seaside I like to think
I hold as fiction. We can never be too naked,
so I ask myself if his suit chaffs at the collar,
if that beach was swept with the chill of long

indifference to cities, indifference festering under
bowler hats in low lit rooms where the art of taking
photographs (imagine the machine)
is as foreign as the skeleton of a stork.

Flies

Grapes left to flies for want
of us sprawled in bed late
are still grapes left to flies. Indifferent,
we must be some riot of guilt, intemperate

loungers, scuffs in the unfinished
threshold of last night. Putrescence
on the lowermost fruit is merely wished-
for grace clothed in ambivalence.

And that you could be holding a glass or held
by one is the same as saying the gelding
lying bloated in the sun, the birch felled
for nothing more than boredom, are seldom

noticed by the mirrors of our house.
The computer hums your name, the flies
some other lust or nonsense of wing. Housed
in their frenzy, beating themselves senseless

against an hour, they know nothing of blue,
nor that their day's so short the bruise
of grapes only keeps in motion two
wings two minutes longer. If they lose

their love of dying, we might also begin
our day as fugitives, like when you swam
off coast with me. The blue-black ocean
held you, and I was dispossessed. Not because I am

a lover of the threat our closeness poses.
I am. Because out of the flies
clouding the bulbs of kelp rose
a gull's riddled body. Something dies

every minute we fail to praise and I care
nothing or very little. What more
can you take from me? I swear
the ocean was once a broken mirror.

Small Deaths

Trapped for days in the bathroom air duct,
it thumped and squabbled, while our window stared
at the stone-choked alley and produce stand

selling squash blossoms I twice fried wrong.
Twice that week, the steady threads of rain
unraveled, mostly drowning out the couple

thin floors, sheets of plaster away. Once,
a lover yelled, slammed the door
and flew the stairs, disbanding pigeons

to some dusk piazza. *Nothing we can do*,
I said, when the sobbing, distinctly male, unwound.
Nothing, too, was what you said one night,

pressing an ear to the door. Earlier, we closed
the bathroom off (we couldn't stand the failure),
and took turns testing the local wine.

Nostos

In the wintry afternoon of our habits, all we love is quiet.
I couldn't say this plainer. Fall falls into itself, television
paints the room in tornadoes and dog food. So little we need,
the lunch meat grows green in its keeper before we decide
how the day burned down. And that night waits on the corner

under an early lamp, plausible, fretting: this is neither
Earth spinning nor some darker revelation, no matter
how many stars stitch themselves into the canopy we built.
The clock spins on the wall so quietly I can hear it,
as I wait for your grope toward the bathroom light,

every night, spelling itself in the space you leave in bed,
as a tornado paints Earth with earth, scours blank Oklahoma
blanker, more receptive. It readies our minds that way.
What follows is merely night on the corner, awaiting
the stern yips of coyotes. Lately you must have seen them

shocking the shorn corner field with their rendering of myth.
Compile, they imply, the tokens of your hatred. Ghastly falsettos
spin upward, the negative of voice, as a tornado turns the Earth
into its twin, more damaged and dangerous for it. Neither are we
hard enough, nor alive to the muscles of our knowing, to know

when a coyote is just that: a promise, a target, night flown free,
the spirals of its eyes recapitulate and savvy. If we were,
we wouldn't keep watching even as evening balances us
on its fulcrum. If we were animal at all, we would grow lazy,
bright in our ignorance, eating ourselves down like saints,

or televised dogs eating food they never asked for. If we were animal,
we would be wild dogs in the streets of Rome. We would strut
around the Jewish ghetto where teenagers kiss and spit at each other,
and we would pause and cock our heads—call it *inquisitive hindrance*—
and we would attack and bite and eat and love ourselves the more for it.

The Divine

Then I warmed the cups and pot,
scalded one teaspoon for you,
one for me, one for the pot,
as if it too remembered, perfumed
in Bergamot. Now after showers,
steam rises from your shoulders.
Knots of leaves scar the teapot bottom
in which to see the future: thin, dissipating
heat in cups, the thinness of your hands—
one cradled, the other fingering the rim's rise,
as I've seen saints in paintings,
and archeologists on TV, palm a skull
and trace the scorched orbitals
where the world enters, where it leads.

Advent

There's a savageness to your sadness,
as I'm sure there was for a scribe
who loved illumination enough to suffer
each flourish. December's clockwork
interlocks around a bookish sun as I watch
you tend to the marginalia your hair makes
around you. And though I'd like one to,
no leaf throughout recorded history has ever
rejoined its tree. The trees, for their part, shake
their nightmares to the ground. True,
the finality of calendars still startles us,
caught in our own largesse. And it's too easy
to say language loves the most meager
of feudal riches, December's needles
a compass mortuary. It would be the same
to say each button on your down jacket
is a rune waiting to be discovered, ruined,
rediscovered, which to some scribe
was reason enough for the opulence
of a fossil moon. We might reinvent the moon
as what our tragic fire aspires to: a hole
in all this sullied constancy. Because no fire
cleanses itself without first dying,
which is why we utter *warmth*: not fire
but the end of fire.

Fever

If sickness is clarity, some magnesium
behind the eyes, Saint Teresa of Ávila,
you understand how skulls end as bowls

from which we feed. You there, swaddled
in camel-hair blankets, yourself a flame,
teach me to burn down this side of sleep,

to rise again. The thin vein of mercury
climbs to 103. Numbers used to make us
shake fists at the earth, sacrifice

dumb animals on blazes. We turned crops
and corpses in their beds to please
the sun, to stop its raining down.

But I've known skies to tremble
over deserts and Japan, Teresa,
explode like money through cities

and lizards in the sand, leave receipts
of living forms on pillowcases, cactuses.
It sweetened meat for days, the fever

sifting into televisions, survivors.
Sickness is a desert where I've returned
to have my mind blown back to this bed

squirming under me. Or if it is my body
questioning why it must consume itself,
Teresa, I give you up for a few degrees

more light, more suns like hot coins.
Teresa, I want to return to the table
of living with an empty bowl.

FOUR

Opossum

In the wasteland of its innocence
without the crudest wall

between itself and the ritual
of boredom and survival,

any wonder night has taught it
reticence? In our inquisitive headlights,

it swallows the little fruits
of sympathy we offer. If we notice

one stiff, turned upward in praise
of midstride, it pleases us

to understand that exodus from living
resuscitates so much

allegory. For here, opossum
lies without the solitude

placentas give, or breasts we cover
because our nakedness would call to us

from when we knew nothing more of God
than what fit inside our mouths.

Dead Swans

In 1912 a thousand swans came down on Seneca Lake to land and
froze to death. Their feet stuck to the ice and they could not take off.
  —Susan Brind Morrow, *The Names of Things*

They must have surprised the small sky
the lake made of their rapture, the squabble
of lesser feathers pursued by reflection,
and have survived too long questioning
their flightlessness, dizzied in the snow fall
each slow death became. Night grew two moons.

For centuries they must have huddled, a page
untouched by ink, while buzzards spun
their cursive promises. For centuries, too,
people ignored them as if a birthing scar,
painless only in its impressionistic study
of flesh, and instead rehearsed a myth

to pin injustice on. Surely a boy's ego
and some bad glue cannot explain
such pointless commerce. The fault, then,
not one of fraud, for who among those
staring lakeside near Geneva in 1912,
or plowing over a museum wall

in Breughel's *Fall of Icarus*—who could
lay a boy at his father's feet and mouth *failure*?
The sin of flight is paid for by the tongueless.
There among girls flocking round the smocks
of mothers, the retrievers' graying flanks,
the chains that must have slackened

and scratched the lake's chrome after each lunge,
among even the very old remaining in the warmth
their own ends purpled the day with, a thousand swans
fell to the ice and stayed there—messengers
in the regrettable business of returning in lump sum
the weight of the sky to all its fictitious owners.

Pseudoscorpion

I caught one magnified on its cathedral
stalagmite, at the Great Basin, in a photo,
enhanced, as if under water, the veined

fish-flesh opaque in its lens-like bell.
The park ranger's Maglite panned
early graffiti, executed, we learned,

by the candle flames of early miners.
A retiree hauls up two summers
spelunking in Ohio, calcified droplets

described as radar pings, until to look up
I thought I was looking down, a casting pool,
rat hole, eye twitching, iris-heavy.

What are the eyes but water welling up, pitched
onto peaks to reflect what was there, no less
strangers than two clumsy hands in the dark?

A killer is loose in Texas, hulled in the belly
of a train. Broadcasts focus on his hands' skill
at wrenching three necks, angling them

like certain pipe organs do the psalms I've heard
too often. Lulled by the U.P. train racketing by
the First Baptist Church, I lie in bed. Evening news

discovers nothing in the ruins of another boxcar fire.
Outside, the live oak races across the window,
faint as microscopic eyes, roving motors into focus,

to a pseudoscorpion, master of the delicate
art of subtraction, its caudal spear lost to centuries.
This emptying of the mind's attic dust:

such is eagerness. I can almost hear the scurry
of train rats, the naked floorboards splintering.
We will know the hand of God by its missing finger.

Beheading Bacchus

The shoulders, lowered in fields, glisten rouge.
Around his head the halo of vines, a fistful
of leaves translucent as skin, a sword curled

with arabesques of the same young flora. Study
the facial muscles. They suggest more than three
hundred heavens, one for every minute

the sun lords over a rain-stained morning.
You've never held the weight of the harvest
knife, strangely heavy, its handle worn,

or felt the deft twist unhinging fruit as a few
seeds hurry to swell the land you walk.
No matter how you try, the painting will not

depart, even after wisps of Giacometti
and an anchor thrown in the courtyard café
where grapes held sculptured poses,

ice clinked in highballs. Later you returned
to Bacchus, grape-stained and cumbersome
in his tableau of tunicked lutists.

Still, he lowers his shoulders, caught in the glare
of a jewel of juice. If he could speak, who's to say
he wouldn't beg? Overripe, he descends to the tendrils

of your engraving. The sun gleams off the blade
you raise. It is late autumn, the three-hundredth heaven.
A breath of wind, buttery and difficult, stirs his curls.

The Death of Byron

Whether of ourselves or prodded, we ended
in a long sloping pasture pocked
with cattle crow-colored but flightless
in their stretched silhouettes. (Flightless

much as Savonarola was but shouldn't
have been: a gash in the day and the terrible
stillness of the day.) Even the lull fell heavy
on the grass as we scouted like grouse

in reeds on shaky lakefronts. Yet you browsed
a certain heifer with avian fastidiousness,
antiquated, deliberate as a flagellant
discovering the boards of his bruising.

The unpeopled landscape was that much more
unbearable after we invented nature.
We picked up our futures, what little we could
find in the rumped commotion of the back-heavy,

while entire pastures, whole heaps, waited for us
where we had come from. Had you looked up then
(I did), you would have seen the moon open its hinges
like a jaw and shut. Shut up. Shut down.

Idol

Twit twit twit
— *The Waste Land*

    Quite the metal,
the sea's afternoon aluminum. Idle trolling
      around Isla Mujeres:
some slack-jaw's rock beach and rococo clapboard
happenings lean to the lean-tos any mind might imagine.
    No one minds
the dock witches cursing seven-foot coyotes, the suicides
of mirrors. Twin kingfishers sleep their halcyon sleep.

    April's perennials:
crucifixion, Cadbury eggs, taxation, spring break.

Thus the beers of Mexico are utopian
—Negra Modelo, Sol, Bohemia—
bobbing in the silken sand, each bottle its own idol
—docile, benevolent, docile—
idle, as each could cause great famine.

    This is why you fish.
Because whales bring down ships
every Ida of the 1890s couldn't pay for
      with such silken ambergris.

Meanwhile, the conch, ratted from the rock,
hunkers in, is no consolation. Oysters swirl in brine,
    a wedge of lime.

Someone wails, *Swallow! swallow!* as you begin
the ageless questioning after the skull's wind,
this gift your tongue makes a hollow thing of.
How can thy heart be full of spring? you might ask
    four frat boys
buoying on the hard deck of the beach disco.
Two hoist a beer funnel as you flick your ashes.
The mind then an open grave, a hull
    cavernous, sconce-haunted.

The one squatting, funneling now—eyes rolled back,
forearms aquiver—lights up in a slow burning vision
    of the eternal topless afterparty.
    Every Ida is there.

Ida, you say, *what is the last whale's language?*
    Swallow, swallow.

The Beginning

They peered at the wonders of the Orient—
precarious gardens, mist around the ankles
of the sacred mounts—and plopped down
their gear. They applied language like a balm
to the indigenous, calmly spreading it along
the contours of the dangerous rivers of faith,
working it between the thighs of monuments,
most of which they found wondrous, possessed,
portable. They left ajar the crypts of pets,
threw caution to the wind, which, to locals,
was a god, though that term was never used.
They chiseled away the jewels of idols,
dismantled their elaborate headdresses,
their disdain for the living. Such work, they found,
was horribly tiresome, so they drank the water,
which they called miraculous, or, if they found
the water possessed, damned with language.
Being what it was, the water said little,
and in a tongue unknown to them.

The Tiniest Green Hummingbird in the World

Its throat feathers (or gorgets)
refracting in the feeder's glare
shimmer as a fly's eyes do.
Hovering, unbiased, being

pin-sized and nonpasserine,
it greets the greatest of your trees
with the cool of the millionth
divide of itself, new-worldly.

The two crows now settling like
battered kettles uneven on
the grape wood, or the woodchucks
caravanning through timothy,

appear distant as continental
shelves, leagues under a strange sea,
some cerulean a bird like this could swim
or fly in. Motionless to any eye

but its own, bejeweled, needle-like
(or, rather, eye-of-the-needle-like),
it stuns with a silence of flight
serving only to keep you praising

its side shift eager as a piston.
If the blisters of its eyes rise
to meet yours, be still. Breathe
in small bursts as to feign

such fluttering. Registering
the smallest fracture of the air
it mastered, the bird will receive
you without the slightest chill.

Or you will pass through,
as you have done each spring
morning through this country
fog-quilted and sluggish,

the geometric necessity
of a tiny thing's nearness
the only fugitive you'd harbor.
Two-and-one-half inches, the size

of a thumb bent thumbing
a sketchbook or, supine, hitchhiking:
this bird and six-foot hum around
some lilac and the world

it's fastened to. Snatch a snapshot
of yourself as you glisten in the bird's
third passing, sugared in red
solution. Good. Developed

in your red room, your prints
display just one pair of wings.
Remember the Continental Divide?
You were the one dividing.

Bird's Eye

1

Blame Icarus. Mock sacrificial rites
in films when the bird the elders believe
the spirit of the dead spirals symbolically

away from the virgin, its view
from above frozen on her the instant
she burns herself into the circuitry.

Next, a speckle of river water, stage blood.
Relegated to the aftermath—
what we glean through narrative or the eye

of a camera—we'd like to squint,
let each pupil insecure and clueless spill
into its iris. Which is why the unworthy

crow torments most with its hidden
seams. Strapped to a mast, for example,
its nest brought the ordinarily myopic

to meditation. Telescoped, horizonward,
we could see for days, literally.
The solitude was enormous.

Nowadays, distant, private bi-wings
thread our canyons, helicopters
scour East L.A. down to the Queen

Mary, even at night the cold, green,
infrared voyeurism, we say,
a bird's eye view. We pay for it.

And why not? The resistance
of retinas tuned like trampolines
to the fidgeting leaf, the cones

shattered in their liquid sockets,
as the sun slips below its lid:
Leonardo knew. If domes, bell towers,

and their patronage kept growing,
we would fly. It's evolution.
In the end, only sketches remain

of his wings, assorted masterpieces,
and his double-helix staircase
for a brothel. After the failure

of flight, he gazed down the throat
of a whorehouse to the famished crawl
of senators, eyes swelling from torch light

and the porno fresco above each door.
Unnerved, Leonardo merely opened
heaven elsewhere. For the wealthy, no need

to wait outside those darker cells where hands
became the eyes' odd sisters fighting
for the right to show the mind who's there.

2

Once, while killing sleep, I kept vigil
by the TV's orbital window, watching
what else?—nature shows. So savvy,

the French with their sparrow silhouettes,
coaching birds away from the cruel weight
of their bodies plunged into Plexiglas

near train tracks. To think: saving birds
from themselves, and off flew the decals
across the continent, peppering the eyes

in passing trains. Poised so contentedly:
one silhouette aiming down as if to dare time
the space between the ins and outs of wheels.

Another straight up, a kind of cross
between a corkscrew and some shot of the old
Dracula actors before imploding

into bats on strings—poof—flattened
in Technicolor or false landscapes of France.
And I've been close. Tunneling blasted mountains

by train, how could I know another
raced toward me—two eyes on a green
monitor somewhere closing the gap.

Then a vacuum, a violent silence
blowing the carriage doors open,
newspapers and curtains hovering

on the same air forced in my head,
into all the passengers, as we sank
back, eyes closed, with a muffled *God*.

All the while, enjoying himself,
the engineer follows the headlight's bulb
until it grows to what the dearly departed

talk about if they return: *the blinding
white light*—they swear—*and a thousand
disembodied souls rushing toward me.*

3

Given time, our eyes lost their double
sense, spent on endless words, on pages
fanned open and meticulously picked apart,

the computer's false fire, or just watching
the late movie with the lights out. Night owls.
That train was the closest I came to a bird-

blind flight into myself. Still, should I worry
about my friends who bird? Scope at the eye,
can't it too allure, prove addictive

like booze or bad fiction, the thrill
of boredom? Once in high school,
I said, *Shoot*, and my friend did,

his one eye centering the crosshairs
on a trivial kill, summoning the lump.
What can I say about the smallest deaths?

In California, then, three things were certain:
higher taxes, Malathion drops, and the persistence
of the famished coyote. Come morning—the disaster

still visible in the dirt—its body was gone.
Curled in their dens, what calls coyotes out?
And how many did we catch in our headlights?

Who's there? We'd ask. *Who cares?*
Half-drunk, half-frightened by our own
bodies and the power they held,

we loved the glow-in-the-dark-skull green
of the coyotes' eyes. And they would,
always, stand frozen for an instant,

allowing night to expand around them—
arched backs, opened throats,
the high-pitched cry of jokers

who pulled one over on us. Or they were still,
waiting for the divine blow to the head,
arrow through the eye we knew they deserved

for the indifference of their nature,
or nature risen to impostor. The moment hung,
immense, just as Julien Gracq described

the Aventine in Rome: *that secret
district where it always seems an eye
is following you.* Of course, nothing happened,

except allegory. And we sat and watched it
burn down like numbers at the start
of a film, waiting for our eyes to adjust.

The Big Spill

You like the fish in its glass whirling
your house around, mouthing Os,

like to scissor hours into snowflakes
with your Windex and your Pledge,

your Hoover hovering above the hardwood.
Life's so finite and clean, you think, you'd eat a peach,

save for the mess. Now picture yourself whirling
in a vacuum, tiny in your hourglass. Recall the black

plastic vacuum's black work after spilling coffee:
no matter how you shaped the hole, the grounds

would not relieve the ground entirely
of blackness. But this house grounds you.

In its finest hour, you think, it's irreducible,
plump as a pit or the hole it leaves with such surprise,

the O opening at the bottom of the fish tank.
O you everlasting, you almost feel the day

dismember, which is why you stop vacuuming.
Your hour has come round at last. Go on.

Each fish bubble is a tanker flooding floorboards
off the coast of Alaska, the big spill.

You imagine harbor guests, on the silent spreading
ocean's black pajamas, saying, *Nighty-night, nighty-night.*